PENNY GANG
A Financial Guide to Success

———————

Born Legend

Penny Gang
Copyright © 2016 by (Born Legend)

All rights reserved. No part of this book may be reproduced or transmitted in any form or by any means without written permission from the author.

Table of Contents

Part One
Set Unrealistic Goals
Write Everything Down
Visualize Your Success
Understand Your Limits
Unlimited Horses
Reading & Math

Part Two
Game Plan
Support Team
Think Things Through
Understand Clear
Accept Change
Have Patience

Part Three
Pay Yourself First
Mind Set
Learn Rules & System
Take Smart Risk
Caught in Your Own Success
How to Stay On

Part Four
Collateral
Stock Market
Borrow Big
Options
Exit Plan
Glossary

A born legend is Abraham Lincoln. Learn to work for one to make two, and the rest is history. Abraham Lincoln is hidden in plain sight and tossed to the ground every day. Pennies become dollars. Forever live Abraham.

"Penny Gang."

Part One

If you're only interested in chasing the almighty dollar, then you're only chasing your tail.

SET UNREALISTIC GOALS

Believe in dreams, because dreams must mean and that meaning has fulfillment.

One must set unrealistic goals when creating a business plan. If you can foresee that a goal is unrealistic, then you can foresee the complications that make your goal impractical. Seeing the glitches allows you the opportunity to repair the issues that make your goal appear unrealistic. Presenting solutions to these problems ultimately makes the goal attainable.

Any goal is attainable with rigid planning and execution. Set many realistic milestones to reach your unrealistic goal; so, if you fall short, you will have still achieved some level of success.
It has been said, "Shoot for the moon, for if you miss, you will fall amongst the stars."

If you always plan unrealistically, life is that much more exhilarating. You will never lose the thrill or feeling you first had when you embarked on your business journey. The challenges, and the craving for more. If you can't stand the heat, get out of the way of the sun, because this fire can't be put out.

What would you name your business?

What type of services or product would you provide?

_____
_____
_____
_____
_____
_____
_____
_____
_____
_____
_____
_____
_____
_____
_____
_____
_____
_____
_____

Penny Gang

STRATAGEM #1

A little girl named Racheal had $3, and so did three of her friends. They each had $3.

Rachel went to the store and bought a toy train for $. She also spent another $1 on potato chips to eat and $1 on a bag of lemons.

Her three friends each bought three $1 toy trains apiece, in different colors. They spent all their monies. Racheal showed her train to her friends, and they mockingly show her all their trains. They laugh at her, because they each had three trains apiece of varying colors, while she only had one.

Rachel leaves and sets up a lemonade stand. At the end of her first day of sales, she had made $2. So, she went back to the store and bought, what? No, not two more toy trains. Rachael bought two bags of lemons and made $4 at her lemonade stand. Then she went and purchased 4 bags of lemons. She made $8 from her lemonade stand and her mother asked her would she like to put some money away. Rachel saved 2 of her $8, and she spent the remaining $6 on six bags of lemons.

She sold out of them and made $12. She eventually made $32. Next, she asked the store owner if she could get more bags of lemons for less than a dollar a bag, being that she was buying in bulk.

The store owner agreed to give her two bags of lemons for $1. The years passed, and Rachel eventually went on to own her own train transit line. She would often see her three friends, riding her train.

WRITE EVERYTHING DOWN

Write everything down. Good ideas, bad ideas, and just ideas in general. Your bad ideas just might become your greatest production, so, don't count any idea out. What's popular today might not be popular tomorrow. Creating a business plan is the best way to achieve success for any goal you set. Be sure to examine every damaging aspect of your plan, and devise a strategy for your best plan. By doing this, you can be comfortable inside your own negative.

People often say, "Don't think negative." Nonsense. You must look both ways before you cross the street, so you also must consider the detrimental and the positive. Negative and positive considered, create a plan for both.

If you don't like to write, record your thoughts on tape, draw them, paint them. The palest ink is greater than the strongest memory! When you brainstorm about your ideas, speak freely, never underestimating an idea. Record it all. Keep writing and talking until it all comes together.

VISUALIZE YOUR SUCCESS

If you can see it, then you can achieve it. You better believe it, nothing is impossible. If you can think it, you can achieve it. If you abandon the word impossible, then nothing becomes impossible. Now, you only must balance your vision. Things that you consider too complicated to understand can ultimately be understood. This will dismiss the complication. Complications are just that; complicated, but not impossible to overcome.

Try to make sense of your timeline. Most people seek immediate gratification and work hard to achieve it, but some of your goals may involve others, whether it be the mail service or vendors. Make time for the things you have no control over. One of the best ways to protect your vision is to have others help you visualize your timeline of events with you.

Listen and learn from other successful people to get a clear picture of the problems that may arise. Then, you can sidestep those problems while you continue to process your timeline. You only must envision it too can achieve it. If you foresee the problem coming, you will be a great problem solver.

Write down 10 Goals you envision achieving.

UNDERSTAND YOUR LIMITS

You must understand yourself. Test yourself with small challenges that may not benefit you, but will build you up. It's like exercise. There is pain involved, but get you healthier, you live better and longer. Practice is the key to perfection.

You must know your limits. You must test your limits and build them up, like muscles. Let's continue with our exercise scenario. Physical fitness involves getting up and doing it, even when you don't want to. When you are struggling with that last pushup, you must get another one in. You must develop great will power.

Knowing yourself and understanding yourself are two different things. For instance, you watch a television, but that doesn't mean you understand how it works.

Understand yourself and your problems. Then, fix matters; if issues continue to arise, you haven't understood your problems. Issues or problems are a direct result of something you failed to recognize or prepare for.

Do not blame others. Use your time wisely and prepare another plan. If you waste time trying to figure out who's at fault, you are wasting time that could be used putting another plan together. You must know where you have been, to know where you are going. Research and study people who are doing what you want to do. Find the best person and the worst person doing what you are trying to do so that you can double your chances of success.

Learn to differentiate your desires from your likes, and needs. You will never have the best of all worlds without stumbling blocks. Both good and bad will each have its day; this must happen for life to balance itself out. -Be sure to know the difference between want and need. If you can live without it, then that's a want. If you will die if you don't have it, that's a need.

Be ready for a change. The way you once did things may not be the way you need to do it today, but several days later, you might need to do it the old way. Don't believe that doing everything the same way will get you the exact same results. Switch it up when need be. Learn to channel every situation to your benefit. Keep changing the station until you find something you like to watch.

Don't regret anything you do or the decisions you make. Keep moving forward and do not worry about the past. Learn from your mistakes. Learn how much you can bear, and improve on it until you can bear anything. Just like exercise, keep building up the muscles that you want to make stronger.

List your business Wants / Needs.

UNLIMITED HORSES IN THE RACE

Putting 16 dogs in the race means that you have 16 ways to win. We can take any noun for this money-making principle and apply it accordingly.

Let's say you bet on a horse race. Your job is to bet on the winning horse. Ultimately, the odds are always stacked against you; more times than not, you're going to lose. So, what are some ways you can guarantee a win?

Try writing down 16ways you can win, and try all 16. That's 16 tries. Planning 16 various ways to accomplish one goal can be a tedious task, but it's worth it. It may not take 16 attempts to win; sometimes you win on the first try.

Whether you win on your first try or your 16th try, either way, you learned. Experience is the best teacher. All steps are good and better than no steps. Remember, some people can't get one step ahead. If you're the one ahead, then you are the winner. Now back to the horse race.

If you did your homework (study) on the horses, you can make an educated bet. If the race has 10 horses on the track, you can invest in 9 of them, 1$ on each horse. If the odds are 10 to 1 on all the horses and you win on any one of the horses you picked, you win 10 bucks. You walk away with 1 dollar, that's a one-dollar profit.

Penny Gang

You have a much better chance of winning with nine horses on the track, especially if you have studied the horses and dismissed the two horses most likely to lose. Now, what are your odds of winning? Always stack the deck in your favor. There is no crime in doing your homework and having more insight than others. Knowledge is power, and power is money.

Penny Gang

What are 16 ways you can accomplish your business goals?

READING AND MATH

These are the two keys; "reading and math." Business law school and accounting school are good ways to further your education. People say, "You are never going to use all that math in life"; these people are limited in their way of thinking. Go as far as you need academically to achieve your success. It does not matter where you start, just start. Do not let pride stop your success from growing and being protected.

Get educated at all cost. Take online courses, or enroll in community college. Whatever you must do to get educated, get educated! Reading and math are insurance. "Understanding" is the name of the insurance company.

Math and reading will always protect you. -If you know numbers and understand the verbiage, you can talk the talk, and run the numbers. Now you're walking the walk.

Stratagem #2

A homeless man once went to work for nothing. He stood in front of a do-it-yourself carwash with only 50 cents in his pocket. A car pulled up to get washed and he offered to wash the car for only $2. He was denied. Five cars eventually pulled up to get washed, and everybody told him no.

At the end of the day, a car pulled into the car wash, and the homeless man went to the driver and said, "Let me pay you 50 cents to wash your car, and if I do a great job, you pay me $5. If I don't do a good job, you pay me $2." The driver wanted to say no, but he admired the homeless man's determination, so he agreed. The homeless man only did a good job, and the driver still paid him $5.

The homeless man realized that if he went to every car like this, he had a better chance at getting work. It worked, he was eventually able to save up $100. He kicked the drug habit and opened a nice size car wash, he now charges $15 to $75 a car. All he wanted was $2 a car.

He said, "One billion pennies is a million dollars, do you think you can reach one billion pennies before you reach one billion dollars, one billion quarters, or one billion dimes, or one billion nickels? Slow motion is better than no motion."

Penny Gang

Call to Action
Start saving your spare change
"Change for Change."

Part Two

First, one must understand that people frequently, almost always, pay more for less. If, it is something they want.

GAME PLAN

You need to have a game plan. A game plan is equivalent to a map or a blue print. As mentioned earlier, write everything down and then you can begin creating your game plan. Your game plan needs to be clear, and straight to the point. It is what you will share with others who can help you reach your goals. Prepare a good plan so that you can present it with confidence. You will be respected and understood.

Over time, your game plan will have to be tweaked and readjusted, but do not despair, because this is normal. It only means that you are growing. Even if the results are negative at the outset, you have still gained knowledge that can be used to orchestrate your game plan. "The reason so many people with degrees fail and don't succeed in their careers is that most of them didn't properly plan all the way through." So, plan, plan, and plan again.

Everything in your business needs to be discussed; what's common sense to you isn't common sense to another. Sing it, write it, draw it, but make sure, your points are understood. Every word has a synonym. There is always more than one way to get an understanding. The key is making sure that there is an understanding.

Penny Gang

Start Writing Your Game Plan.

Stratagem #3

How can I make ten cents ten thousand times? In effect, turning ten cents into 1000 dollars. Chris became an entrepreneur in prison. He was selling single cigarettes for 1dollar apiece, yet, his competitors were selling single cigarettes for 4 dollars apiece, due to supply and demand. Why did Chris sell his single cigarettes for $3 less? Chris had taken the same $4 cigarette, and broken it down into four individual, smaller cigarettes.

Then he created a small-loan service. While most charged $1 on the $1, he would charge $1 on every $2. In this way, he began to extinguish his competitors. How many ten cents was Chris making now? He eventually reached 10,000 dollars. He used the profit to expand his business. Next, he started selling store commissary. His competition was loaning out $12.50 in commissary for a $25 repayment. Two for one. Chris did one better, he loaned $15 --in commissary for a $25.10 return.

Penny Gang

Now, the dimes were coming in at breakneck speed. Before he knew it, Chris had profited $1,000. He bought a car for $500 while still in prison, and then rented it out to the family members of the people incarcerated with him so that they could drive to prison to see their loved ones. They paid him top dollar for an eight-hour rental. Chris bought three more cars while incarcerated, and rented them all out. He was soon making $500 a week just in his car-rental service. He then began seeking more investments.

Name Three 10$ hustles you can start.
1.
2.
3.

SUPPORT TEAM

Your support team is your fans, and you have home-field advantage, but you must be able to sell tickets to your fans. Be willing, by any means necessary, to go the extra mile for your support team. "Fans" are equivalent to friends, family, and anyone along for the ride, good or bad. Your support team helps you to understand where you want to go, and where you need to be.

Make sure your support team has similar goals to yours, and are willing to go the extra mile, just like you. Always be aware of your fan's needs. Let the business be theirs, and let them have input and say to how the company is run. Allow them to write the rules inside the rules. Set lengthy processes for changing what is a law. A lengthy process means the law will remain intact for an extended period.

Consider the Government's processes; to change a law takes an eternity. These processes are designed to be a headache. Before anything concrete takes place, --most will just give up. It's a "buy-time" strategy. Your support team should be the ones that you love, trust, and are willing to forgive. Don't pressure your team; too much pressure creates a fear of failure. This leads to deceit in most cases, and deceit can destroy dynasties. Make sure your team's goals and your goals are aligned.

Penny Gang

Name *your* support team members.

THINK THINGS THROUGH

Think ideas all the way through. Then ask yourself, what can derail your plan? --When you figure that out, make another plan. Always have a plan for your worst knock down, and be prepared. The only sure way to be ready is by thinking things all the way through. Plan for the unexpected.

Ask the opinion of others, but do not let them discourage you. Use their ideas to help you think your plan all the way through. Opinions of others often include their thoughts on your demise. Great! Use this knowledge to your advantage, and move forward. You already know all the positive benefits of your ideas, so there is no need to waste any more time getting another person's thoughts on that.

UNDERSTAND CLEAR

Listen before you speak. Always make sure you have a complete understanding during any conversation concerning your business. ---Ask questions, and say you don't understand if you don't understand. It's better to have a good understanding than a bad one.

When negotiating, make sure the conversation is on your level of understanding. Don't be prideful and misunderstand due to intimidation. Speak up, and let it be known when you don't understand. Everyone has different levels of understanding; no level is better than yours. If all involved have an understanding.

A doctor may say, "cardio-arrest." A computer tech may say, "mother board destroyed." A drug dealer will say "a drought." Fundamentally, they are all saying that something is severely damaged.

ACCEPT CHANGE

Create a change day once a month, and have your associates tell you what they think you can improve on. Change the problems before they change you, and change accordingly to achieve your success.

Ask, why is this a problem? If your associates can't communicate why a problem is a problem, then it's not a problem.
Learn to accept change, because it's coming. You will have to change some things more than once.

Always have an open mind, and try to make sense of everything.
 "Constant change is here to stay, provided nothing changes."

Penny Gang

Name 16 ways to improve yourself for business.

HAVE PATIENCE AND BE HUMBLE

Patience is everything in all situations. You must have the patience to see your plan come to fruition. Patience is imperative because you will always have to wait on something or somebody at some point and time in life.

Practice as many times as you can, a trillion times if possible. Practice until you become the greatest. Practice means doing it repeatedly.

Humbly explain to all your associates that you will be preoccupied with personal business. Some people will want to be involve d in your plans and some won't, some can't be involved, and some should be involved. Remain humble when explaining this to all individuals, needed or not needed. Being humble can be a useful tool. Smile and wait for your moment, because it's coming. Also, when success comes to pass, be humble still.

Stratagem #4

A person pawns a cell phone for $50 at a pawn shop. The pawn shop wants $62 back in thirty days or they keep the phone, the phone is worth $175. It's the middle of the summer. He takes the $50 and invests it in bottled water. He takes the water to the park and sells all the bottles at $1 a bottle. He walks away with $100.

He has a light bill that's due for $100. He holds off on paying the light bill and purchases more bottled water. He turns the $100 into $200. Then he pays the $100 light bill and the $62 pawn shop bill. It's summer time; bottled water sells like, well, bottled water.

There are a million other penny investments out there that you can sell and flip. Now, what about the $38 profit? Reinvest the $38 in bottled water, and then invest in other ventures like juice. You started with nothing, and now your investment vehicle is still growing based on the $38 profit that you may have flipped 100 times.

Now you can build up your portfolio and credit. The more investment vehicles you accrue, the closer you are to your goals. Pennies add up, and so do investment vehicles. Always have multiple ways to profit. There are plenty of investments that are safe or with little to no risk. It is up to you to do the thinking and the work.

Penny Gang

Select one $10 hustle you will implement this month.

Part Three

Never argue with another person's theory. It's their theory, they are leaving out or adding what you are not understanding. Listen to that person's views, and then thank them for their time.

PAY YOURSELF FIRST

Look to invest in someone else's plans, if they are willing to cut you in on the profits. Look for as many no-loss investments as possible. They do exist. Make sure it exists by doing your research on the investment.

Learn how to save. The first step to saving is knowing what you can afford to put up. If it's 5 dollars a month, that's okay; invest it in vehicles like 401K's, IRA's, banks, etc.... This is not the money one uses the first time a problem comes up. Only tap into your savings as an absolute must. Sometimes there are fees for borrowing against your own money. Look for good reasons to dig into your savings, like other investments.

The second step is to save money. Pay yourself first, which is putting up your savings first. Always looks to save something.

Stratagem #5

There was a very smart lady who loved chewing gum. So much so, she wanted to make her own chewing gum. She did her research, and then she invested $20 for all the supplies needed. From her $20 investment, she could produce 5000 pieces of one cent chewing gum. That equaled out to $50 and a $30 profit. She became a success in her community, to the point that a major chewing gum manufacturer learns of her success and sought to buy her recipe.

It wasn't the fact that she was successful that these major manufacturers sought her recipe; it was the profit achieved from her recipe. She was making more chewing gum from less money.

Penny Gang

Savings Plan.

How much are you paying yourself first each month?

MIND SET

There are two ways that your mind has been conditioned. One way is through the public eye, or, the world's way of living. The second way is the private way, which is your way of living, that has not been made public.

Your business is only truly complete once you understand both minds sets because they are both beneficial to your success.
The public conditioning plays with a fixed coin; it has its own side, and the other side is your side. Your private conditioning is a fixed one-sided coin. It is imperative to become a two-headed coin or you won't succeed.

Modify all that you have learned. Identify all that you haven't learned, then implement it into your business plan. Learn how to make the financial gain off both sides of the coin, appeasing both the public and yourself. Learn to modify and identify the patterns in everything business.

LEARN RULES & SYSTEM

Learn the rules to anything you're involved in. Never jump into anything head first without knowing the rules and having a game plan. Your livelihood is on the line with every decision you make, from the smallest to the biggest decisions. Make the rules and understand them. Rules are the key in everything. Play by the rules until you can change the rules.

Change the rules to your advantage. You must follow the rules that are already in place to be successful; there is always an "order of operation" to everything. There are even rules to doing nothing.

Rules make the system. --Whoever has the power to make the rules creates the system. The beginning of changing a system is by changing the rules. Every entrepreneur has his own God. The people they employ are the Christ.

First, find out what people need and create the job. You put the rules in effect to make sure your business stays running. You will have to learn the system first, become a part of it to understand it, then you can use it to your advantage.

Penny Gang

There are a billion ways to make money. Ultimately, it's the system that keeps the money coming in. The people working the system make you money.

TAKE SMART RISK

Take calculated risks. Break everything down to its lowest common denominator. No matter how long it takes. Remember, no doesn't mean you have failed. No means that you must find another way in. Don't let words trick you into giving up. A, yes is always possible with the right calculation and moves.

Only go as far as you calculated. Then plan and calculate again. It's too risky to just jump into something past what you have planned. It's never a waste of time to double-check yourself and repeat the cycle until your path is clear. Only go as far as you can foresee the future, with as much clarity as you can possibly muster. When you see the clarities end, execute what you planned. Then think, plan, and implement your next plan.

Name three calculated risks you can take to increase profits.

1.
2.
3.

CAUGHT UP IN YOUR OWN SUCCESS

Never get emotionally caught up in the business, deals, or the problems that arise. Always analyze from diverse angles. You can never have enough plans. Stay sharp, stay thinking, even after you achieve success. There is more than one way to succeed.

"It's success even if you get caught up in an unsuccessful quest."

A wise man once said, "You are succeeding by failing. You are succeeding at failing."

You can relish in your success, but don't get lost in it. The high of success can cause you to become lax; one slip can cause you to lose everything. **Work hard not to succeed at failing.**

HOW TO STAY ON

Repeat your strategies as many times as needed until you achieve your success. After this, understand the art of marketing and promotions. This is a crucial key to a business's success. Understand your target audience, your customers. They are the judge and jury, so you must make them happy.

Keep asserting your investments in every good deal, and never rest.

1) Continually plan and study.
2) Keep investing.
3) Market your business to your target audience. Then feed your audience good product.
4) Stay loyal to your customers.
5) "Plan for a Rainy Day"

Invest in a plan that saves you money, (401K or IRA). Invest in valuable real estate, CD's, art, coins, or another business. Only make a deal if you can get out what you invest; no matter what. It is imperative that you get out what you put in, and that your money can earn money.

Penny Gang

There are always ways to receive loans for collateral. Use your investment items as emergency monies. Whoever you leave your items with as collateral, always make sure the company or person allows you a guaranteed way out with your original money or product investment. Otherwise, do not invest with them.

Essentially, you are preparing for the day you encounter an unforeseen event. It's inevitable, but if you stay patient and move strategically, the sun will never stop shining.

If you plan correctly, you will never have a rainy day, and even if it does rain, make money off the rain.

Name three rainy day plans.

1.
2.
3.

ROB PETER TO PAY PAUL.

Peter is Bank of America, and Paul is SunTrust. Let's simplify this. Borrow $10,000 from Paul, then use this money to purchase an asset. Let's use a car, for example. Then go to Peter and ask for a $10,000- loan against your car. Then take the $10,000 and pay off Paul, then you can sell the car for a profit. Or you can keep the car, and use it to turn a profit. Uber, car rental, etc....

With the profit, you can pay Peter and kill the loan. Or, as another option, you can ask Paul to borrow another $10,000. You can repeat this cycle a million times, and maximize off your profits.

Is it worth one hundred tries if the goal is worth achieving? If you try one hundred times, then you have 100% odds of winning.

Does it really add up for you? That's what counts.

Part Four

Know your competition. Know how far your market is going to go in any business. Know how many people are willing to buy, or need to buy. When you have the thing a person wants, they will pay for it.

COLLATERAL

Insurance, gold, silver, art, cars, houses, land, business, products, etc....

You should always be able to borrow from your investments. Look at all your assets; remember, you can borrow from what you own, whether it be a pawn shop, bank, or title company. You can always get a loan for your valuables.

Do not to use the money that you borrow on anything that you owe. Only use the money to invest on something you know you can make money from. Then you can use the profits to pay debts.

STOCK MARKET

Every noun can be considered the stock. You can choose to go public with your stock if you like, but consider what going public means. Going public is essential letting the government in on your business. Why would you do this? When you allow your stock to be sold publicly, the entire world becomes your market place, but you must allow the government to have a say in your business venture. Essentially, you and your business become stock.

There are pros and cons to going public. Going public has great short-term benefits, and can be a gigantic stepping stone. The con, there is no room for mistakes, you can certainly lose everything due to no fault of your own.

Every and any noun can be an investment, and you can make money. Investments are like vehicles; no matter the vehicle, car, truck, motorcycle... they are all means of getting one to a specific destination. Multiple means of transportation equal multiple investments, all essentially traveling down the road to success.

A stock is a supply of goods. Goods are items, items are product and product is money. You must be shrewd when choosing what to invest in. You must know what stocks are good for you, and the ones that are not. More importantly, you need to know how to make money off them all.

Remember, when you want to invest in something, ask yourself, is it putting money in your pocket or taking it out?

A stock market is the market place that holds a count of all the goods and services, which is a product, which is a business. Money is a money-making machine.

When you take your company public, then you open yourself/business up to the public. So, plan and obtain a qualified person to help you in all your decision-making processes. The stock market is a giant flat-screen TV, showing everyday money business. It's all a gamble!

It's like attending a horse race, except you place bets on what you think is going to happen with companies and businesses. You can bet on companies going down, or you can bet on companies going up. You win if you pick right.

The stock is, and has control over, selling the shares that a company produces (goods). Money is the product that Stock sells. They sell by borrowing money to grow a business, and the return to the buyer is a "share" of the business.

Simplified, you borrow $20, they want $21 back. Stock companies keep up with your monetary progress and invest (bet) on your likelihood of success.

This is an organized way for the government to watch how much money is made by various companies, and the government watches its own money by taxing every dollar. Investing is like taking a lengthy car trip. You are traveling ten thousand miles, but your initial vehicle will only get you the first one hundred miles. You still have 9900 miles to go. You sell your first car or rent another with more miles per gallon to finish your trip. Go the extra mile.

Stratagem #7

There is a cartoon about a cat, a dog, and a bird. The cat is always trying to eat the bird, but the bird always finds a way to escape. The cat never stops trying and has even caught the bird a time or two, but he only played with his food and the bird eventually gets away again. This is because the bird never stopped trying to get away. The dog stays out the way until the cat gets in its way.

This is about persistence. As we grow older, we tend to forget what it is to be tough. Which character are you? Are you the dog? Laid back, well feed by its owners, and taking it easy? Or are you the cat? Always busy with the same focus. Or are you like the bird? Innocent and constantly fighting for your life. Keep your cartoon youth! Become the Cat, the bird, and the dog.

Which one are you right now?

- ❖ The Bird
- ❖ The Cat
- ❖ The Dog

BORROW BIG AND BREAK DOWN

EFFECT:

Your big bringing down is going to go back up because of your multiple investments. What you invest in should bring in a greater return than what you have borrowed.

Whatever you choose to invest in should be worth more than what you invested.

You buy a house for $35,000, it should be worth $40,000 or more. Profit can also be made in renting the home out. Then you buy more houses.

Notice, now you are making money before you buy borrowed monies.

OPTIONS

The powerful cannot thrive without options. You must keep all your options open in the business world. If a person says, "They don't want to buy," ask, what will make them want to buy?

See if you can implement that need and still achieve a profitable gain. --Always remember: something is better than nothing.

OPTION O.P.M.:
One of the best options in the world is to use another Person's Money. Learn to use another person's money.

OPTION REDUCE:
Reduce any debt incurred by borrowing from something you own that's worth more than all your debts. When borrowing, always try to pay it off as fast as you can. If you need the money again, then borrow again. This is an ideal way to build credit and credibility.

Always think big, and bigger. Once you're at your biggest big, the one that's so big that every time you aim you hit it, then you can begin taking aim at the smaller big. Every time you hit your target, you get rewarded.

EXIT PLAN

It's good to have an exit plan, for the day that you exit the world. Invest your money and business in something or somebody that can help your legacy live forever, to keep helping and building up the world. Donate money and assets to a charity of your liking, and leave the businesses to your family.

Have your plans in order, and put them on paper, so that all parties can see it, copy it, and teach it.

Penny Gang

What is your exit plan?

Penny Gang

Final Stratagem

The track:

Borrow $500 to make a $1,000. Now, what will you do with the $500 revenue?

Place the initial $500 back into your original product to make yet another $1,000. Seek another $500 loan and put that with the $500 in revenue to make $1,000. Invest the $1000 in a different product. Now you're making money.

Now you are ready to invest in a store front. Your business plan calls for a $20,000 start up. Borrow $20,000 from a bank, and purchase your property; your property should be worth at least $30,000.

Find another bank and take out a greater loan; let's say $30,000 because the store front is worth that. Buy another property worth more than $30,000 and rent it out at a profit.

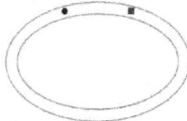

Borrow yet another $60,000 from the new property in which you paid $30,000. Then you pay off the $20,000 you owe the first bank. Your initial $500 investment should be doubling as it had from the very beginning. Use this money to pay off debts and interest rates.

Now, with the $60,000 house, borrow $90,000 and purchase more properties.

Then borrow $150,000, repeating the cycle or circling the Track.
Then pay off the $60,000 loan and buy more property.

Borrow $170,000, and buy other properties, and then borrow 250,000 for other properties.

Then borrow $400,000, $600,000, $800,000…….
Now, you're at $1,000,000. Repeat the track.

It must be said, that you must make money before you circle the track. If you can't capitalize on an investment, then you cannot circle the track.

Take the story from your head, and create your own exciting and descriptive novel. We can write your story for you!

Yourstoryhere.biz
www.bornlegendoperatingcompany.us

Penny Gang Vocabulary Words

Asset- Property owned by a person or company regarded as having value and available to meet debts, commitments, or legacies.

Bond- A binding agreement. An obligation made binding by a money forfeit.

Broker Firm- Arranges contracts for property in which he or she has no personal interest, possession, or concern.

Capital- Stock or surplus earnings that are free of debt; especially capital received for an interest in the ownership of a business.

Certified Certificate of Deposit- Written recognition by a bank of a deposit, coupled with a pledge to pay the deposited amount plus interest.

Common stock - Stock other than preferred stock.

Dividend- An individual share of something distributed.

Equity- The money value of property in excess of claims, liens, or mortgages on the property.

Equity Financing- Selling a percentage of ownership in the company to an investor.

Firm- A partnership of two or more persons that is not recognized as a legal person distinct from the members composing it. A business unit or enterprise.

Fund- A sum of money or other resources whose principal or interest is set apart for a specific objective.

Hedge- A means of protection or defense (as against financial loss).

Hedge Fund- An investing group usually in the form of a limited partnership that employs speculative techniques in the hope of obtaining large capital gains.

Income Bond- A bond that pays interest at a rate based on the issuers earnings.

Inflation- An act of inflating: a state of being inflated.

Junk Bond- A high-risk bond that offers a high yield.

Liability– sums of money owed; debts

Monopoly- An economic advantage held by one or more persons or companies.

Mutual Fund- An open-end investment company that invests money for its shareholders in a usually diversified group of securities of other corporations.

Peace Dividend- A portion of funds made available for nondefense spending by a reduction in the defense budget.

Preferred Stock- Stock guaranteed priority by a corporation's charter over common stock in the payment of dividends and usually in the distribution of assets.

Promissory Note- A written promise to pay at a fixed or detainable future time a sum of money to a specified individual or to bearer.

Revenue Bond- A bond issued to finance a specific project, the income from which will be used for repaying the bond.

Revolving Fund- A fund set up for specified purposes with the proviso that repayments to the fund may be used again for these purposes.

Savings Bond- A nontransferable registered United States bond issued in denominations of $50 to $10,000.

Share- Stake in the ownership of a company.

Sinking Fund- A fund set up and accumulated by usually regular deposits for paying off the principal of a debt when it falls due.

Slush Fund- A fund raised by a group for corrupt practices, such as bribery or graft.

Stocks- Security issued by a corporation representing ownership rights in the assets of the corporation and a right to a proportionate share of profits after payment of liabilities and obligations.

Stock Broker- An agent in the buying and selling of stocks or other securities; a broker.

Stock Certificate- An instrument evidencing ownership of one or more shares of the stock of a corporation.

Stock dividend- The payment by a corporation of a dividend in the form of shares usually of its own stock without a change in par value.

Stock Exchange- A place where security trading is conducted on an organized system.

Stock Split- The stock distributed in a stock dividend.

Surety Bond- A bond guaranteeing the performance of a contract or obligation.

Trading Company- A company that is financed with capital invested by the members or stockholders who receive transferable shares, or stock.

Treasury- The place of deposit and disbursement of collected funds; especially: one where public revenues are deposited, kept and disbursed.

Treasury bond- A long-term bond issued by the U. S. Treasury.

Treasury note- A currency note issued by the United States Treasury in payment for silver bullion purchased under the Sherman Silver Purchase Act of 1890.

Trust fund- Property (as money or securities) settled or held in trust.

Yield- To give up possession of on claim or demand.

NOTES

www.ingramcontent.com/pod-product-compliance
Lightning Source LLC
Chambersburg PA
CBHW050015230526
45470CB00003B/971